Wedding Planning Made Simple

Wedding Planning Made Simple

An All-In-One Wedding Planner

Bryan and Marian Box

iUniverse, Inc.
New York   Bloomington

Wedding Planning Made Simple
An All-In-One Wedding Planner

iUniverse books may be ordered through booksellers or by contacting:

iUniverse
1663 Liberty Drive
Bloomington, IN 47403
www.iuniverse.com
1-800-Authors (1-800-288-4677)

ISBN: 978-1-4401-2060-2 (pbk)
ISBN: 978-1-4401-2061-9 (ebk)

Printed in the United States of America

iUniverse rev. date: 1/21/2009

Contents

Introduction

Congratulations, you're engaged! But what do you do now? Where do you start? Married couples are probably bombarding you with their ideas, thoughts, plans or suggestions and you may be feeling somewhat overwhelmed. Where should you begin, what reference materials do you require, in what order should things be done, what is your best source of information, and finally is this book any good for you? With **Wedding Planning Made Simple** we are presenting a tool that simplifies and organizes your wedding preparation details. Our goal is to relieve the stress and anxiety while saving you both time and money by making use of principles couples before you have used.

We want you to have the wedding you have always dreamed of and strongly believe in the saying that if you, "fail to plan," you are "planning to fail." While this may seem harsh, the intent is simply to stress the fact that with proper planning and realistic expectations, the chances of achieving your goals increase dramatically. This theory applies not only to your wedding, but to all aspects we undertake in our lives.

We, Marian and Bryan, (the authors and creators of this program), enjoyed a 7-year long distance relationship. We were separated by about 2400 km and yet made it to the altar. So you see, long distance relationships can work, and you never know you just might create a product together. Being separated by this distance and trying to plan a wedding required the use of email and spreadsheet files to track all of our particulars. What evolved is of course our creation of this book and the on-line wedding planning software for other couples to use to plan your own weddings. We wish you all the best of health, happiness and success as you begin the next journey of your lives together.

Wedding Planning Made Simple has been created as a multi-faceted planning tool and is a secure website, https. Each chapter begins the same way. Both Marian and I share some of our thoughts about weddings, *('She says' and 'He says'),* followed by an explanation of "What needs to be done," to plan your wedding. This section is a lead into the, "How it gets done," aspect of planning a wedding. In this section, we outline how to integrate your wedding planning with the on-line portion of this program that is included with your purchase. Think of this section as an elaborate instruction manual with examples to guide you to the wedding of your dreams. If you wish, read the first section of each chapter and when you are ready to access the planning tools use the second section of each chapter to guide you.

Throughout this book we will reference a fictitious couple, Karen and Tim, using a Wedding Planning profile created using PlanningMadeSimple.com. Using Karen and Tim's wedding plans,' we will highlight the features of, and show you examples of our program. So let's get started.

They registered for their On-Line Wedding Planning program and began their planning by accessing, **www.planningmadesimple.com.**

From the home page of **planningmadesimple.com** you will notice a tab called, 'Clients'. Click this and simply enter your personal login and password information. The following screen appears;

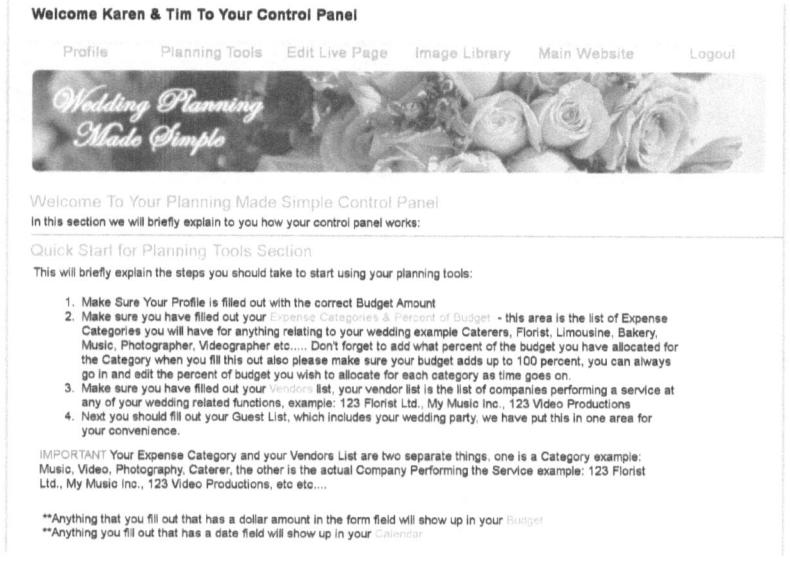

(To register for your own on-line program which is included as part of your purchase of this book, including your own webpage please reference **Appendix D – Accessing & Setting Up Your On-Line Program**)

You will notice a, **"Quick Start for Planning Tools Section."** This is an excellent refresher once you begin using the program.

The following explains the Menu Buttons and Sections of your new Wedding Planning Program;

Profile

The Profile Button allows you to edit your contact information. From here you set your budget, personal details, your username and password.
Parts of the information in your profile will show up on your free wedding page, for instance the "**Bride's Name**" and "**Groom's Name**" fields show up the header portion of your template and the "**Date of Wedding**" will show up in the footer part of your template. If you are unsure of your wedding date simply leave it blank.

Planning Tools

The Planning Tools Button is where all your wedding planning begins. There are **Budget forms, Guests, Vendors**, **Events, Gifts, Expenses**, **Calendar, Contacts, Diary, & Template** sections, each one designed so you can view, edit, add and delete information as items arise.
There is also a complete explanation of how to use each of these tools in their respected links. Look for the pink question mark and click on it if you require assistance.

Edit Live Page

From the *Edit Live Page Button*, you tailor your live wedding website, which will be visible for all your friends and family to see. You can add links to maps, directions to events, i.e. rehearsal dinners, photo sessions, bridesmaids, dress shop, etc... the sky is the limit.
Editing Your Live Webpage is a simple process accessible from your control panel;

- Just click the "**Add Paragraph**" link to add your paragraph of text. Once you have added your text you can then insert an image corresponding to that text.
- Use the "**Image Library**" tab and follow the instructions to place an image in with your text. Once you add your images a simple dropdown list populates allowing you to pick the file you want.

To add more paragraphs simply repeat the process above.

Image Library

The Image Library Button allows you to add images that you want to display on your free webpage.

To add your image, simply click on the;
- "**Upload Image**" link, a second window opens which says "**Please Upload your image**"
- Click on the "**Browse Button**" then browse to the image you wish to upload.
- Once you find your image highlight it in the window then click the "**Open**" Button.
- You should now be back at the screen you started at, click on the "**Upload**" Button and your image will be uploaded.
- Click on the "**Back**" link and you will see your new image in the image library.

Main Website

The Main Website Button as the name suggests brings you back to the main website. If you haven't logged out, clicking on the "**Client Area**" Button brings you back to your control panel without having to re-log in.

Logout

The Logout Button logs you out of your control panel and takes you back to the main website. Once you log out you must click on the "**Client Area**" Button from the Main Website and add your login name and password.

Now that we have you introduced to our truly "All-in-One" Wedding Planner, we're ready show you why this is the only tool you will need to plan your dream wedding.

Best wishes with your upcoming nuptials.

Chapter 1
Getting Started

She says...

One of the first things Bryan and I did after our engagement on December 20th, 2003 was select a date. Since we were in different cities, (never mind different Canadian provinces), we wanted to pick a date that would accommodate everyone we wanted involved. While we had determined that the wedding would be in my hometown, we also had to consider things that the guests on Bryan's side could do while having to travel to another province for the wedding. As a result, we invited all out of town guests to the rehearsal dinner as well as the day after lunch/ gift opening.

We also knew that we didn't want the wedding on a long weekend. We both agreed that we had spent too many long weekends at other weddings and we were not going to inconvenience anyone by having ours on a long weekend. Ultimately we decided on August 6th, 2005. This allowed me to finish my university classes and attain my second degree, give our traveling guests time to plan and pay for the trip, plus afford us the time to plan a wedding that we would be pleased with.

He says...

As you begin to envision your ideal wedding I want you to keep these three questions in mind.

1. What is important to you?
2. What is important to your guests?
3. What do you want people to remember?

Quite possibly the answer to these questions right now may not be the same, but if you allow yourself to plan realistically your Wedding Legacy will be one that will satisfy all three. Think of these questions when you make decisions on the particulars of your wedding. Do you need more centerpieces on your table, or would that money be better spent on an extra item of food for your reception? Your guests want to have a good time, you want the party to be fun and you hope that your friends will talk afterwards that they really enjoyed the evening. They probably will not discuss how many decorations you had on the ceiling or where the special flowers were located in the reception hall. In other words, plan your dream wedding but be conscious of what people take notice of, and you just might end up not spending as much as you thought you would.

You will probably begin to see a pattern in my one page synopsis of each chapter that I am budget conscious. While I understand that you &/or your spouse wants everything to perfect, comments such as, 'what is an extra $100', can be the comments that lead to running up and possibly over-exceeding your budget. I believe you can have a perfect wedding without breaking the bank. While you do not want to seem like scrooge to your partner, you can discuss your requirements while still taking into consideration your finances. As I am sure you have heard before, 'it is one day vs. the rest of your lives'. So leave a little in the bank to enjoy your honeymoon and new lives together.

Getting Started - What to do.

While the thought of planning your wedding may seem daunting, a simple trick is to break down the event to smaller tasks. If you remember the saying, 'you can't see the forest for the trees,' you will be well on your way. In other words don't focus so much on every detail that you lose sight of what is really important. This is precisely what we have done in this wedding planner. Below you will see the different aspects required to plan a wedding in separate categories. As you progress through each step, you will begin to see the entire picture come together while not feeling overwhelmed by thinking everything needs to be done at the same time. You will have access to each of the Planning Tools listed below. A brief overview is presented here which will be developed in more detail in subsequent chapters.

The Wedding Planning Tools

My Wedding Budget

Track all of your expenses with your wedding budgeter broken into categories representing typical wedding expenses. You pick your budget and categories and the program calculates the estimated costs for each category. As you add your true expenses, a running total is produced indicating if you are on track to reach your projected budget or if you are over or under in certain categories.

My Wedding Vendors

Keep track of all the vendors that are involved in making your wedding go off without a hitch. Add as many vendors as you need, or view all their details at a glance.

Expenses for all your wedding planning including Gifts & Favours

Organize all details of gifts and favours, such as attendee gifts, wedding party gifts, welcome gifts and parting gifts. Keep records on all of your wedding expenses, hotels, food, flowers, transportation, even your engagement party. This portion includes any and all expenses related to your wedding.

Wedding Accounts Payable

Keep track of your vendors, by address and phone numbers, the total amount owing to each vendor, whether deposits have been made, and what dates they require final payment by.

Wedding Guests & Contacts

Wedding Guest List

Create an organized guest list that will keep track of all of the details of your attendees, who is coming, who is not, who is tentative and their contact information. Print a list of all attendees and their contact information so you can easily address invitations. Columns are also available to indicate if they have sent you shower gifts, wedding gifts and if thank you cards have been sent.

Wedding Party

Create a wedding party contact list. Use to designate tasks or 'to-do' lists for the wedding party members for any events such as the engagement party, rehearsals and wedding day.

Wedding Contacts

Contacts include all your guests, your wedding party, and your vendors.

Wedding Gifts and Thank you Cards Organization

Create an organized, 'Gift List', filtered by wedding gifts, registry gifts or shower gifts, with columns indicating if thank you cards still need to be sent out..

Wedding Event Checklists

Wedding Day Emergency Kit

All the things you need in case of emergency, extra pantyhose, ties, hair clips, duct tape etc.

6-12 Month Checklist

The countdown has started. Our convenient countdown calendar will help keep you on track of your wedding planning details and when they need to be done.

Wedding Related Events & Event Checklists

This area is where you put in your engagement party, your ceremony and any other event that goes hand in hand with your wedding.

Wedding Party & Guest Tasks

Here is where you designate tasks for each event with people involved in the wedding. As long as they are in your Guest List, you can designate a task for them for any of your events. It will also show up in your calendar if you give it a date.

Wedding Seating Plan

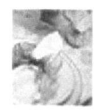

This is the ultimate tool in which you are able to create your own personalized seating chart! Our print function allows you to print the seating chart, so you can give to your reception coordinator. It's extremely user friendly and exactly what you need to tackle the seating chart task.

Wedding Flowers

Add flower arrangement details, special requests, *example white roses tipped pink*, print the page and use as a checklist to ensure completion.

Wedding Caterer

Plan the food and beverages for your Rehearsal Dinner, Wedding Dinner, Reception or other event you are having.

Wedding Photography and Video

Use this file to keep track of your photographer and/or videographer's contact information, as well as to create a list of the individual, couple, and group shots that must be taken on your wedding day. Cuts down on the stress the day of the wedding if the photographer simply ensures the required pictures are checked off the list.

Wedding Music

Keep a record of your music preferences and create a list of the music you want played (and not played) at your wedding.

Wedding Gifts & Thank you card list

Has a card been sent for shower or wedding gifts received, was the gift a registry item etc. All these items organized in one handy place.

Organizers & Calendars

My Wedding Calendar

Organize your, 'To-Do's, with an updated calendar in which you can print and post as a reminder for what you have to do for the day/week/month.

My On-Line Wedding Diary

We included a template where you can simply write whatever you feel you want to remember about the planning of your wedding. This makes a great keepsake when the wedding is over.

My Wedding Registries

Keep a list of your gift registries, by store or by area of the house, and have easy access to them whenever you need.

The Little Extras

Wedding Contract

Protect yourself. We have provided a standard contract form that you can use when negotiating and purchasing services. Simply input the requirements of the supplier and the negotiated pricing and timing and feel more secure. If your proposed vendor doesn't want to use this guarantee, maybe you have the wrong vendor.

For the Do-It-Yourselfer, Print Your Own Wedding Invitations, Reply Cards, Ceremony Programs etc.

Save money by printing yourself. We have included templates from standard stationery stores, (Michaels', Staples, etc.), that you simply input with your details, buy the stationery and the hassle of setting up the print area is taken care of. Save hundreds of dollars, not to mention hours of fighting with printer settings.

Free Wedding Page

Share the steps leading up to your wedding, add pictures, & links to maps and locations, itemized events. Example: rehearsals, dinners, wedding schedule, wedding locations and more.

Getting Started –Here's how you set it up.

If you are ready to jump right into using the program, the following is a Quick Start guide. If you haven't set-up your Planning Website yet simply email us at planning@planningmadesimple.com and give us your name, spouse's name and wedding date plus proof of purchase.

Quick Start for Planning Tools Section

This will briefly explain the steps you should take to start using your planning tools:

1. Make Sure Your **Profile** is filled out with the correct **Budget Amount**
2. Make sure you have filled out your Expense Categories & Percent of Budget - this area is the list of Expense Categories you will have for anything relating to your wedding, for example your Caterers, Florist, Limousine, Bakery, Music, Photographer, Videographer etc..... Don't forget to add what percent of the budget you have allocated for each **Category.** When you fill this out also please make sure your budget adds up to 100 percent. You can always go in and edit the percent of budget you wish to allocate for each category as time goes on.
3. Make sure you have filled out your **Vendors** list. Your vendor list is the list of companies performing a service at any of your wedding related functions, example: 123 Florist Ltd., My Music Inc., 123 Video Productions
4. Next you should fill out your **Guest List**, which includes your wedding party,

   IMPORTANT Your **Expense Category** and your **Vendors List** are two separate items, one is a **Category,** example: Music, Video, Photography, Caterer, the other is the actual **Company Performing the Service,** example: 123 Florist Ltd., My Music Inc., 123 Video Productions, etc....

Anything that you fill out that has a dollar amount in the form field will show up in your **Budget
Anything you fill out that has a date field will show up in your **Calendar

** There are individual help files for each section, look for the question mark and click on it for help relating to that screen.

Chapter 2
Our Wedding Budget

She says...

Booking a photographer is an important part of having a great wedding. Pictures are the one thing that you see and distribute after your wedding so you want someone who will listen to you and who can show you their portfolio. My sister had a wonderful photographer for her wedding, (she was married 2 years before us,) and I wanted to use the same person. Bryan didn't care so much about who we had as a photographer but more concerned about the cost. I called my sister's photographer and he honoured my sister's price which was a steal considering some other quotations we received. Plus, we got to keep the negatives so we could get any photos developed, whenever we wanted without the photographer charging extra. (Big Plus!) I was satisfied to have this task booked.

Bryan on the other hand didn't think we were getting such a great deal. In order to get through this and get the photographer I wanted we had to create a budget. We made a list and decided how much we wanted to spend in total. In order to reach our target budget of $10,000, we created categories of spending and assigned each category a percentage. This way, we could compromise in different areas in order to get what we both wanted without going over budget – almost! When the final tally was in, having done some things ourselves to save money we wound up being about $1,100 over budget. It was worth every extra penny!

He says...

One Saturday afternoon Marian called me all excited to tell me that she had found a photographer for us. I was primarily interested in the cost and if we had already given a deposit when she informed me that the photographer was the same company that her sister had used two years prior and that they were fantastic.... All I wanted to know was how much. Marian couldn't believe how good a deal we got. She said it was only $1000.00 and they would even take some pictures during dinner. I just about fell off my chair. I asked her how she could spend that much on a guy who takes pictures when everyone we know will probably have a digital camera there anyways. As I later found out through my own research we did actually get a pretty good deal. What I did learn, other than what your are probably thinking anyways, that I should just listen to my wife to be, was that, when you are looking for a photographer (or any vendor for that matter), of course shop around, but perhaps you know someone who was recently married and loved their vendor. When Marian called the same company that did her sister's wedding she mentioned that her sister was impressed with her pictures and what price they had paid for them. What this did was show a sense of allegiance and probably forced this company to give us preferred pricing as we knew what they charged just two years ago.

The Budget - What needs to be done.

While perhaps not the most exciting element of the wedding planning process the details of your 'Budget' and preparation of it are paramount to the success of your wedding. Creating and sticking to your budget are of such importance that we have dedicated a substantial amount of information in this chapter to it.

Weddings are expensive, but there are many ways to accomplish your goals without breaking the bank as they say.

How do you decide on your budget? Remember the three questions from Chapter 1. It is very easy to overspend if you do not know beforehand what you are looking for. A wedding is a major expense and the financing of it is different than some of the other large purchases you will make in your life. Take for example purchasing a vehicle, you will usually have up to five years to pay it off if you would like. How about a house, 25 even up to 35 or 40 years to finance homes these days is not unheard of? However your wedding will probably have to be paid off by the day of your wedding or possibly as late as one month after your wedding when your credit card bills are due. For these reasons, the wedding plan is very important and there are certain considerations as you prepare your budget.

Sources of Cash

I don't believe that you should go into debt when planning your wedding. To avoid this you need to know what the sources of cash will be and then set your budget to come in below this amount. You could perhaps even plan on spending at a level up to 10% below your forecast so you have some wiggle room if problems arise. How much money will you and your fiancé be able to contribute? How much will you receive from your parents/grandparents, relatives? Will you include monies that you assume will be collected the day of your wedding from your guests? *While it is not a good idea to assume a certain amount from your guests to be used for budgeting purposes, you can use an estimate if you wanted to from your guests to cover honeymoon expenses.*

What is going to be included in your budget?

Would you like to have an open bar, elaborate transportation, a violinist or your honeymoon included? Once you have determined some of these bigger issues you can start to prepare your budget.

The on-line Planning program included allows you to enter the expense categories and percentage of your budget you would like to use for your wedding. Some suggested categories would be;

Category Name	Percentage of Budget
Reception/Food and Beverage	40
Wedding Attire	10
Stationery	10
Flowers & Decorations	10
Photography/Video/Music	10
Gifts, Fees. Miscellaneous	10
Honeymoon	10

Of course you will want to enter your own categories, decide if the honeymoon is to be included or not, but whatever categories you want to include, be sure that the total of your percentages is 100%.

We would be remiss if we did not include some TIPS for purchases that we observed in our own wedding planning.

Negotiate, (for everything) and Use a Contract

Don't just accept the price from a supplier. Get at least three quotes. If you really like one store but you think they are a little expensive, use the, 'hum, ah and stall technique', and say that while you like this item you also like the same item from ???, and they are 10% less. You never know. (10% off your $1000 dress is $100 more for you). Do not be afraid to ask for discounts when you are ordering a large volume of a particular item.

Contract

We feel very strongly about having a contract with your vendors. So strongly we included a copy in your planning tools. Get your purchases in writing. A simple form can be filled out between you and your vendors to provide that extra level of comfort when you make your large purchases. Your wedding dress is a great example of when a contract should be used. We have all heard the horror story of the dress not arriving on time. With a contract you specify when the item is required and the penalties of late delivery. Most vendors will not want to lose money and a signed contract can help ensure that your conditions are met. In our opinion, if a vendor does not want to use a contract to provide you with the security of their promise, perhaps you have the wrong vendor.

Contract Tips &Suggestions

Elements of the Contract

Necessary items:
- Legal operating name, address and contact info of the vendor
- Legal names of the bride and groom
- Date and time that the required item is necessary. (if you are unsure of the exact date and time, simply add a statement indicating that the date will be added and agreed on by both parties.)
- Services &/or products should be listed with all particulars associated with each. More detail is better than less, add supplemental sheets if you have to.

For Services:
- Set-up time, start, finish, and break-down time should be listed
- Name of the person or persons who will be performing the service
- Any delivery of products after the wedding (such as photographs or videos) should be listed, with a date by which you will receive the product.

Pricing and Payments:
- Exact amount should be stated, plus any additional charge related to that expense so that there are no surprises later.
- List each item included with a particular price. (Do not be afraid to use extra paper. Have you ever seen a small legal document).
- If there are set-up or breakdown fees for a particular item, make sure the details and pricing are included with the contract. You don't want to be surprised later.

Taxes and payments:
- The contract should indicate whether taxes are included or not. You don't want a 15% surprise.

- Include a schedule of payments, due dates and penalties, including the forms of payment acceptable, and applicable penalties (for example, if a personal cheque is returned).
- Also, include penalty clauses on your vendors in the event they breach the contract.

Use Supplemental sheets

- Use supplemental sheets if required. Now is not the time to leave out the small details. You do not want to give the vendor an out by simply not including everything you want.

Terms & Conditions:

- Termination clauses and their details should be included. Can either party terminate, penalties, reasons timing etc?
- If the vendors have their own terms and conditions, make sure you read and change, negotiate or alter portions of their contract that you see fit. You do not have to accept their terms just because they have them. Negotiation implies compromise. Do not be bullied by seemingly legal jargon.
- Make at least three copies of the contract. One for you, your vendor and a witness, with original signatures. Any amendment should be initialized on all copies by all parties.
- If the contract lacks any of these items, don't hesitate to request corrections, additions or verification of details. It is in everyone's best interest to have everything listed in advance. If the vendor hesitates to provide you with a detailed contract, perhaps you should consider a different vendor.
- By ensuring that you have a valid contract, listing as many specific details as possible, you can feel more relaxed regarding your vendors as you approach the big day – and better safe than sorry!

Policies:

- Cancellation policies should be included in the contract, with specifics regarding cancellation by either party.
- If there are other relevant policies that the vendor follows, they should also be included in the contract.
- You should be presented with an original copy of the contract, with two sets of original signatures—yours (or the person responsible for paying) and a legal representative of the vendor. In order to make the contract binding, you will need to present compensation at the time of signing.

- If the contract lacks any of these items, don't hesitate to request corrections, additions or verification of details. It is in everyone's best interest to have everything listed in advance. If the vendor hesitates to provide you with a detailed contract, perhaps you should consider a different vendor.

- By ensuring that you have a valid contract listing as many specific details as possible, you can feel more relaxed regarding your vendors as you approach the big day—and better safe than sorry!

The following form is included for reference and is part of your on-line program. Simply fill it out and print it off.

Wedding Contract
Between

_____

&

_____

Vendor's Address: _____

_____

_____

for the Supply or Service of:

_____

_____

_____

This contract represents the agreement between the above mentioned parties for the services and or products mentioned above. The following list indicates the requirements of both parties for completion of said contract;

Item	Vendor Requirement	Delivery Date	Cost $ (incl. taxes)

Special Circumstances; _____

_____

_____

_____

_____

Bride/Groom   Date:

_____

Vendor   Date:

_____

Witness   Date:

Wedding Contract
Between

_____

&

_____

Vendor's Address: _____

                         _____

                         _____

Supplemental Information:

(Ask these questions of your vendor so there are no surprises later. Delete this line when you print this sheet. Tailor the items below to you own personal needs.)

Hall:

Smoking Allowed?
Parking/Overnight?
Capacity?
Tables?/Round/Rect.
Head Table Skirting?

Who cleans up?
Time bar closes?
Corkage fee?
Insurance?

Air Conditioned?
Additional Fees?
Guests/Table?
Table Linens?
What time do you have access?
Decorations down by?
Bartender Provided? Cost?
Bring own alcohol?
Liquor license?

Caterer:

Tablecloths/skirting?
Seconds Offered?
Guarantee hot food?
Caterer cut and serve cake?

Buffet/Homestyle/Waiter?
Wine served by Waiters?
Staff wear/Uniforms?
Time of dinner/late lunch?

Some More Purchasing Tips

Shop Around

In essence, shopping around is negotiating. (The Internet can be a valuable source of research.) Schedule a meeting with potential vendors and you will probably receive better service. Ask to see a sample of their products, such as tasting the food. There are a lot of stores in the wedding industry that will be more than happy to gain your business, so be sure to ask for what you want.

Watch out for the Knick Knack's

These are the, 'oh this is cute' $50 purchases that you never end up using. Make your plan, decorations etc., before you purchase your items. It doesn't take very many small purchases to add up to a big expense. I would guess every married couple has a box of really cute, 'what were these for', that they never used. *(I know we have one)*

Keep Receipts

This goes without saying. Hopefully you won't need them but.....

Use Credit Cards

This is another good way of protecting yourselves. While I suggest you should only purchase items on your credit card if you have the money to pay them off, the credit card trail does provide some level of security should something with your purchase go wrong.

Check and Double Check

Verify what you have ordered and that the quantities are correct. If you are having invitations printed, make sure you order extra as it is more expensive to do a partial order later.

Remember it is One day vs. the Rest of your Lives

Have Fun

Relax. If you have planned everything beforehand, the execution will flow smoothly. Plan before, so you enjoy the day of.

Some other wedding cost savings tips you may want to consider.

Consider the day

Friday evenings and Sunday afternoons are becoming more popular. Most suppliers will offer discounts for the off-busy days. You may even find discounts on spring/winter weddings.

Limit Your Guest List

Do you really know everyone attending your wedding? While your parents may feel you have to invite certain people because of… remember it's your day. Or, make that an item that your parents pay for.

Photographer/Videographer

Use the referral technique. As we mentioned earlier, maybe you have had a sister or friend use a vendor a few years ago. You can always say, 'you did Sarah's wedding two years ago for about $750. I thought the pictures looked really good and she got to keep the negatives'. This puts pressure on the photographer to charge you less than the going rate. They may be charging $1200 for pictures these days but they will feel obliged to ask for less, maybe $1000. If you're really lucky they may offer the same rate.

Some people opt to use family members to do the photos and video. Remember though, they are there to witness your wedding and they may not feel as though they want the pressure of recording the events. Do not force your wishes upon them.

It does save money but remember this person will not really get to enjoy your wedding the way other guests do.

Some couples have asked their guests to use their digital cameras and take pictures of whatever they felt like and then have them sent to the couple. You may be surprised how willing people are to do this. You get some great photos and actually some better candid shots than a professional would get. It may even turn into a competition between guests about who gets the best photos.

Invitations/Reply Cards, Envelopes, Ceremony Programs

You can save hundreds of dollars by printing invitations yourselves. With home based printers, computers and graphics programs you can create the same look for a fraction of the price. Remember what people do with invitations. They look at them quickly, write down the date, maybe put them on the fridge and look back at them the day before or day of the wedding. As long as your information is clear, neat and concise, what else do you want from them? You can buy the stationary from craft or business stores in bulk and a couple of printer cartridges and you are done. For $300 (stationary and ink), you can probably do 150 invitations, (~300 guests), reply cards, envelopes and maybe even a very nice Ceremony program.

As it turns out, we included templates for you to print your own should you wish.

Use the Internet

While not for everyone, you can save money by having people RSVP you through e-mail. Some guests you may have to call, but it is an idea if you are so-inclined. You can also have your information on a website for others to view.

Wedding Cake

Buy a small but elegant cake for the pictures and serve your guests a regular sheet cake. (They won't notice the difference)

The Dress - After the Wedding

Have you considered having your wedding gown preserved and stored properly? You never know down the road who may want to use your gown again, *(a daughter perhaps,)* but regardless as we stress budgeting why not preserve the one item that consumes a significant portion of your capital. A great resource to help you with this can be found at weddinggownspecialists.com.

The Budget - How it gets done.

To set-up and control your budget you will make use of the following *Planning Tools.*

Budget, Vendors, Expense Categories and Percent of Budget, Individual Expenses

(You may find having your Wedding Planning website open will make it easier to progress through the instructions. The shaded sections are simply how the instructions are viewed on your on-line page.)

By now you should have entered your Wedding Budget from your Profile Tab. If you need to make a change, either access the Profile tab, or change it directly from the link found in the Budget tool under "Change Budget Amount". Of course, don't change your
Budget amount to satisfy your increased spending, instead, monitor your spending to stay below your Budget.

Profile

This is where you:

- Edit your profile
- Add or edit your budget amount
- Update or change your wedding date
- Change your password.

To begin entering your Budget particulars…

Budget

Now that you have set your budget amount in your **Profile** area,

- click on, **Budget or the Budget Icon,** (from the Planning Tools tab), and look for the link that says **"Change Budget Amount"** should you wish edit or change your budget amount.
- The "**Individual Expense Category**" on your planning tools page populates all your budget information.

NOTE - Make sure you have filled out all your **Vendors** and your **Expense Categories** before you attempt to do your Individual Expenses. **Again, make sure your categories add up to 100% for an accurate forecast.**

To create your budget using your expenses there is a specific order in which you need to enter your data.

1. From the, "Create your Expense Categories and Percent of Budget", simply enter the categories you wish to include in your budget and the percent to allocate to this category.

Expense Category & Percent of Budget - Plus Registry Categories

This is broken into two areas.

- **Expense Categories**
- **Registry Categories**

Expense Categories

In this area you add all your different **Expense Categories** and what percent of the budget they will take up, example **Limousine Service** or **Videographer** or **Photographer** and what percent of the budget you would like to allow for these categories.

How to add a Budget Expense Category

- click on the **Add Budget Category** Button, a box will pop up asking you for a **Category Name** and **Percent of Budget**, if you aren't sure just fill out the Category Name, you can always come back and add the percent of budget later,

- click on the **Add Category Name** Button, now you will see your new category under the **Budget Categories** heading. You can edit or delete these at any time.

Please make sure your categories add up to 100% for an accurate forecast.

Sample Category List

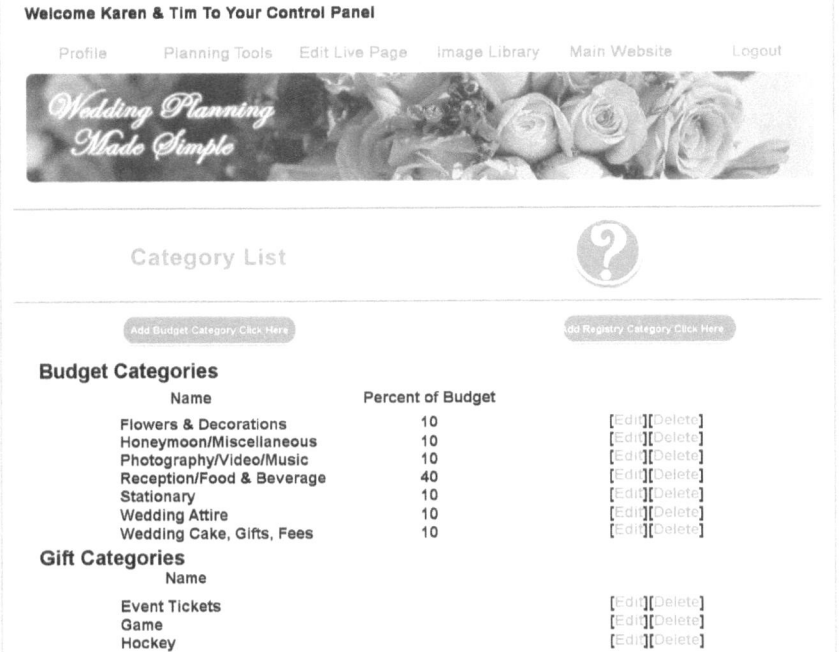

2. Next, "Create Your Vendors". Icon visible from the Planning Tools tab). If you are unsure at this moment of your vendors, simply use a placeholder such as, 'All-in-one-store', which you can change later. Any information you enter for your vendors will be visible from the, "All Contact Icon". (A great way to track everyone's information).

Vendors

Vendors are all the suppliers that will be providing you with items for your events, like your **Wedding Reception**, your **Wedding Ceremony**, your **Engagement Party** etc....

In this area you add a vendor, which then populates the main vendor page. Once you see it on the main vendor page you can edit or delete this vendor. You can also add any notes you need to keep track of about this vendor.

From Karen and Tim's panel you will see their vendors.

Welcome Karen & Tim To Your Control Panel

Profile   Planning Tools   Edit Live Page   Image Library   Main Website   Logout

Vendors

Add Vendor Click Here

Name ▼▲	Phone	Email	Command
Jay's Video	555-555-555	you@youremail.com	[Edit][Delete]
KD's Flower Shop	555-555-555	you@youremail.com	[Edit][Delete]
Michael's	555-555-555	you@youremail.com	[Edit][Delete]
Photos by Dawn	555-555-555	you@youremail.com	[Edit][Delete]
T&G Catering	555-555-555	you@youremail.com	[Edit][Delete]
Val's Bridal Shop	555-555-555	you@youremail.com	[Edit][Delete]
Waterloo Rec Centre	555-555-555	you@youremail.com	[Edit][Delete]

3. Use the "Individual Expenses" icon when you want to enter any particular purchase. It should be apparent now why we first entered information for our vendors and expense categories. For each expense, click add expense,

    • enter the category it belongs to, (a pull-down menu was created when you set-up your Expense Categories),
    • select your vendor, (another pull-down menu),
    • enter the expense value,
    • if a deposit was made,
    • when the payment is due
    • if there is an associated task with this item.

You will notice that any information you enter that has an associated dollar figure will populate in the Budget file, and anything that has a date assigned to it will be tracked in the calendar section of this program. This becomes a very convenient tool in that all of your tasks and who they are assigned to can easily be printed off for guests and family helping you with the preparation of your wedding.

Individual Expenses

NOTE - Make sure you have filled out all your **Vendors** and your **Expense Categories** before you attempt to do your Expenses.

Adding an individual Expense :

- description

- vendor

- category

- total amount - (shows up under budget)

- amount paid so far - (shows up under budget)

- deposit

- delivery date - (shows up in your calendar, anything with a date will show up in your calendar)

Don't forget to update your payments made on your expenses, under the **Edit** link

Sample Expense List

Welcome Karen & Tim To Your Control Panel

| Profile | Planning Tools | Edit Live Page | Image Library | Main Website | Logout |

Expense List

Add Expense Click Here

Expense	Vendor	Actual Cost	Payment Due	Command
Balloons	KD's Flower Shop	400.00	2007-01-21	[Edit][Delete]
Dinner (150 people)	T&G Catering	3300.00	2007-01-21	[Edit][Delete]
Flowers for Ceremony	KD's Flower Shop	200.00	2007-01-21	[Edit][Delete]
Veil, Shoes	Val's Bridal Shop	300.00	2007-01-21	[Edit][Delete]
Hall Rental	Waterloo Rec Centre	1500.00	Not Set	[Edit][Delete]
Invitations & Reply	Michael's	150.00	Not Set	[Edit][Delete]
Photography	Photos by Dawn	1200.00	Not Set	[Edit][Delete]
Video Ceremony	Jay's Video	350.00	Not Set	[Edit][Delete]
Gown	Val's Bridal Shop	1500.00	Not Set	[Edit][Delete]
Ring	Emery Jewellers	2000.00	Not Set	[Edit][Delete]

Screen shot showing the Add/Edit Expense

Welcome Karen & Tim To Your Control Panel

Profile   Planning Tools   Edit Live Page   Image Library   Main Website   Logout

Wedding Planning Made Simple

Add/Edit Expense List

Expense Description	Flowers for Ceremony
	Add Vendor
Vendor	KD' Flower Shop
Total Amount	Flowers & Decoration
Amount Paid	200.00
Deposit	0.00
Delivery Date	2007-07-21
Date Due	

Update Expense

Back

4. You can view your expenses two different ways, from the "Budget Icon" or from the "Accounts Payable Icon". All of your pertinent information with regard to payments can be found in the accounts payable spreadsheet. You can update this when a payment has been made or an action item completed. You will notice that the program will acknowledge a completed item as well as once the balance has been paid.

Accounts Payable

Group By: Category   Filter By: Update Expense

Flowers & Decorations

Expense	Vendor	Cost	Deposit	Amount Paid	Amount Left	Complete
Headtable Flowers	Val's Bridal Shop	$200.00	$0.00	$0.00	$200.00	No
Flowers for Hall	Val's Bridal Shop	$300.00	$0.00	$10.00	$290.00	No
Wedding Party Flowers	KD's Flower Shop	$190.00	$0.00	$0.00	$190.00	No
Flowers for Ceremony	KD's Flower Shop	$200.00	$0.00	$0.00	$200.00	No
Balloons	KD's Flower Shop	$400.00	$0.00	$40.00	$360.00	No

Photography/Video/Music

Expense	Vendor	Cost	Deposit	Amount Paid	Amount Left	Complete
Picture Frame	Michael's	$40.00	$0.00	$0.00	$40.00	No
Photography	Photos by Dawn	$1,200.00	$200.00	$200.00	$1000.00	No
Video Taping	Jay's Video	$350.00	$0.00	$0.00	$350.00	No

Reception/Food & Beverage

Expense	Vendor	Cost	Deposit	Amount Paid	Amount Left	Complete
Cups 1	Val's Bridal Shop	$200.00	$0.00	$30.00	$170.00	No
Hall Rental	Waterloo Rec. Centre	$1,500.00	$0.00	$300.00	$1200.00	No
Dinner (150 people)	T&G Catering	$3,300.00	$300.00	$0.00	$3,300.00	No
Gift Bags	T&G Catering	$200.00	$10.00	$0.00	$200.00	No
Napkins	T&G Catering	$200.00	$0.00	$50.00	$150.00	No
Water	T&G Catering	$300.00	$0.00	$50.00	$250.00	No
Coffee	T&G Catering	$300.00	$0.00	$100.00	$200.00	No
Tea	T&G Catering	$200.00	$0.00	$50.00	$150.00	No

The budget is as simple as that. Remember to update often, and be conscious of how each individual item you buy affects your overall forecast. Tracking all of your expenses is a great way to manage not only your wedding finances but your finances in general.

When most people are asked how much they spend in a month, they usually underestimate the true amount. This can be a result of feeling ashamed possibly of what they have spent their money on, or simply forgetting everything that occurs throughout the month. Write it down, log it using Excel© files or whatever you choose as your method, but do not overlook your spending or debt will inevitably follow.

Chapter 3
Wedding Party and Guests

She says...

Bryan and I agreed we would have 4 attendants on each side for our wedding party. I knew right away that I wanted both of my sisters and the two friends I have know the longest, (one since age 3 and the other since age 7). This was an easy decision for me. Bryan on the other hand had a really difficult time selecting his attendants because he had been in so many weddings with friends and family. He was torn between choosing family or friends for the groomsmen. As I would agree to 4 attendants' maximum, Bryan couldn't include both his three brothers as well as his friends. Finally, we agree to include his friends as the Emcee and ushers, and his brothers as the groomsmen. This was a great compromise for Bryan and I, and everyone included. Friends come and go or these relationships can last forever, but family is always forever.

He says...

'Did you know it has been more than twelve years since we have seen Uncle Terry and Aunt Cathy? I'm not sure if we have even met their youngest two kids. They have to be invited and don't forget about Cousin Jackie'. Does this sound familiar? Your parents telling you who and how many of their friends should be invited or that Steve should be invited because he is a close business associate of your father and it would help strengthen their relationship. Stop! Remember this is your wedding, and while you may get financial assistance from your parents, essentially you are the ones paying for your wedding so at the end of the day you should decide how many people are to be invited and who just doesn't make the list. As Marian mentioned I have been in about 10 weddings and best man for three of my friends. I did have a decision to make about how to include everyone in our special day. By having my brothers stand with me and my friends as greeters and the emcee I accomplished what I wanted. Marian summed it up best by saying that, 'family is forever', and remembering that this was our day we decided how we wanted to have our wedding remembered. As I discuss later, by communicating with everyone you want included, most decisions become easier to make.

The Wedding Party and Guests - What needs to be done?

Bridal Party

Remember this is your day so you decide how many people are in your wedding party. Even if you have been in numerous weddings do not feel obligated to ask everyone you know to stand with you. As a couple you need to decide on your; Maid/Matron of Honour, Best Man, Bridesmaids, Groomsmen, whether you are having Ushers, Flower Girl, Ring Bearer or a Trainbearer(s). These are some of the people who you are going to rely on to help you organize your wedding so take their personal lives into consideration before you ask them. Possibly your best friend has moved too far away to help with the everyday details, or one of your attendants is pregnant and not comfortable standing. Whatever your decisions are, be upfront and honest with whomever you select or do not select and use your good judgment.

Wedding Guests

Similar to deciding on how many attendants you will have, you must decide how many people you wish to attend your ceremony, whether they are included for the entire event, or just the wedding and/or reception. Your budget should help you determine roughly how many people you invite. Do not feel obligated to invite everyone you know. If it makes it easier, limit your parent's to a certain number of friends, limit the numbers from your places of business, decide on how many cousins, nieces and nephews should attend. If you had a choice between a pretty good meal at $25/plate, (for 174 people), or a really great meal for $29/plate, (150) people could you narrow down your invite list by 24 people? While our intent is not to make your event simply a cash conscious affair, we are reminded of the original three questions, one of which was; 'what do you want your guests to remember?' We speak from experience as we received many unsolicited compliments on our meal from both a quality and selection point of view.

Organizing the invitees

Don't re-invent the wheel, and the KISS method, (keep it simple smart guy), are just a few of the cliché's that I can think of why you would make use of a spreadsheet program to help with your wedding plans. One of the biggest disadvantages we found when using one of the numerous planning books on the market in our own wedding planning was in their hard copy nature. Once you write in them they can't very well be re-used. The very nature of a spreadsheet program that employs all that computers have to offer greatly improves your flexibility and can save you enormous time and energy doing repetitive events. With a spreadsheet guest entry program, you simply enter your guests' names once and then you can manipulate the program so that you never have to re-type anyone's information. The use of the CSV file, (included in your program), allows you to send everyone on your list an email by just using the copy and paste features similar to MS Excel©. In addition, when printing envelopes for your invitations you can set-up the program to print onto standard labels you might find at stationary stores. With a few copy and paste clicks you can print 30 labels in seconds and never have to re-type anyone's address.

At any time you can refer to the 'All Contacts' icon for the complete address list of your wedding guests, wedding party members and all of your vendors and suppliers. You can also filter this file to just show wedding guests or vendors if you wanted to print a specific list.

Of course after you have mailed (or emailed if you are in cost-saving or environmental mode,) your invitations and begin to receive your replies, the program allows you to enter if a particular guest has sent in their RSVP and how many are attending.

Wedding Party and Guests – How are you going to organize it?

To organize and maintain your Bridal Party and Wedding Guests information you will make use of the following *Planning Tools*.

Guests/Wedding Party, All contacts

Guest List

This is where you can add your guest list and the people in your wedding party.

By clicking on the "**Add Guest**" Button you

- simply fill out the form,
- check if they are in the wedding party or not,
- if they are, type in their title, for example **Bridesmaid** or **Flower Girl**

and the program takes care of the rest. For guests simply type in their particulars.

Come back to this area when your guest has sent you their R.S.V.P.

- click on the "**Edit**" link next to the guest name and check the R.S.V.P. box "**Yes**",
- then click the "**Edit Guest**" Button to update your guest.

You can also delete a guest from the list by clicking on the **Delete** link under the heading Command

Once a guest has been added going back to the main guest page will allow you to edit or delete your guest, change them from a **Guest** to **Wedding Party** member or visa-versa.

Actual file as it appears on Karen and Tim's webpage to add/edit a guest.

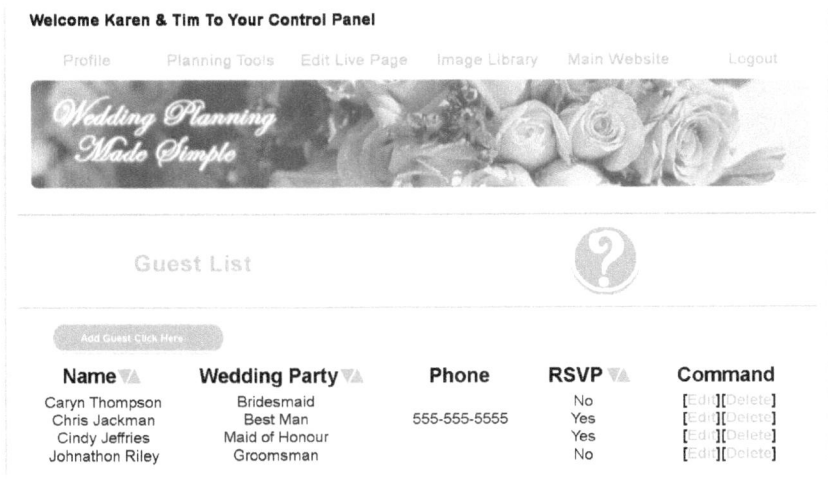

Welcome Karen & Tim To Your Control Panel

| Profile | Planning Tools | Edit Live Page | Image Library | Main Website | Logout |

Add/Edit Guest

Name:
Street:
City:
Province:
Postal Code:
Country:
Phone:
Email:
RSVP: Yes ○   No ○
In Wedding Party: □
Wedding Party Title:

[Update Expense]
Back To Guests

Your guests and wedding party are then assembled into chart form, the arrows allow you to sort the names.

Welcome Karen & Tim To Your Control Panel

| Profile | Planning Tools | Edit Live Page | Image Library | Main Website | Logout |

Guest List

Add Guest Click Here

Name ▽△	Wedding Party ▽△	Phone	RSVP ▽△	Command
Caryn Thompson	Bridesmaid		No	[Edit][Delete]
Chris Jackman	Best Man	555-555-5555	Yes	[Edit][Delete]
Cindy Jeffries	Maid of Honour		Yes	[Edit][Delete]
Johnathon Riley	Groomsman		No	[Edit][Delete]

To view all of your guests or vendors simply refer to the "Contacts" icon from your planning tools. You can print each category individually if you wish.

Contacts

This section lists all your contacts including your **Vendors, Wedding Guests** and **Wedding Party.**

You can display all your contacts at once or display them by **Vendor, Wedding Guest** or **Wedding Party** using the filter feature in case your lists get too long. Clicking on a contact allows you to directly update them.

Chapter 4
Events and Their Checklists

She says...

I LOVE lists! Bryan on the other hand HATES them. So when we started planning, I did what comes naturally and staring making lists. Essentially they were passed on as Bryan's 'To-Do' lists. The numerous spreadsheets found on many websites are fine although I found that I wanted to make my own to suit my own needs. Many of these standard lists have things that you need to do that might not be a part of your wedding. For example, my mom made the bridesmaids dresses, so I didn't need to worry about any of the items that involved bridesmaid dresses in the checklists. Also, we didn't have a formal engagement party so we excluded all the planning details from our lists and added extras for the rehearsal dinner. For these reasons, we specifically designed our program to allow you to create your own action items.

He says...

I guess Marian mentioned my sentiments on lists and that I always enjoy knowing what needs to be done around the house. That being said we did create a series of spreadsheets to help you stay organized.

This chapter essentially represents the 'nuts and bolts' of planning your wedding. Every detail that you need to consider can be found somewhere in this section.

As an example of where some planning may have come in handy. I was the best man at a fall wedding about 4 years ago. The ceremony was held late afternoon and everything went off without a hitch. The plan was to have the bridal party walk down the aisle, outside into the waiting garden and then go in the back door of the church while the attendees filed out. The idea was that everyone would see the couple leave, the guests would then exit the church and the couple would walk back down the aisle and go outside to be greeted by the guests who would of course be waiting. No problem, right? When we got back inside the church, the minister was already in shorts and a t-shirt ready to go home for dinner and standing there with his hand out. The groom looked at me with a bit of a stunned look, leaned over and said is there any chance you have $400 on you. I need to pay the minister and I forgot to bring a cheque for him. Of course I did not, so I casually went about the crowd of guests gathering $20 here and $20 there and eventually we were able to get the minister home for dinner, albeit a couple of minutes later than he expected. Of course, with a little pre-planning the groom could have avoided an eye role from his bride of ten minutes.

Events – What needs to be done?

The hall has been booked, now we just need to decide who is performing the music, when is the photographer showing up, are we getting a video done, who is going to sit where…..., you get the picture.

There may also be events along the way leading up to your wedding that may require some degree of organization. Socials, stags, bachelorette parties, stag and does, showers and even family get-togethers, are just any of a number of events leading to the actual wedding itself. We took the liberty of having the *Wedding* set as a default event that requires planning, but with *Wedding Planning Made Simple*, you are able to add any event you want to that may require varying degrees of planning.

It is within the, '*Events and their Checklists*' planning tool that all the requirements that you have probably concerned yourselves with come together. As luck would have it, we have the templates in place for you to manipulate. You will notice on the program, spreadsheets for the photographer, videographer, musician, caterer, florist, tasks and even a seating plan.

Some of our thoughts on these particulars;

Photography – We touched on this in the introduction. Photography can be a significant portion of your wedding tab and somewhat rightly so. This is the documented memory of your wedding and every effort should be taken to make sure you get it right. That being said, you don't need to break the bank to get some pictures taken. Shop around, use some of the negotiation tactics we explained in Chapter 1 and don't be afraid to ask for what you want. Make sure you control your negatives. You don't want to be upended when you discover that you have to pay extra for a particular pose you like.

Our program comes into play when you are working with you photographer. It has been known to happen that the wedding can become a little frantic and some items may get overlooked. You don't want to have to put your dress back on the next day because you forgot to have a picture taken with your family. While this may be an over-exaggeration, the theory behind planning ahead of time is a sound one, and any opportunity you have that can remove uncertainty and stress, will diminish the possibility of being disappointed afterwards. For this reason, we included a template that you simply fill out with the pictures you want to have taken on your wedding day. Think of the pictures you want to have taken before, during, and after the ceremony, at special places to the both of you, certain people you want to be remembered with, at the dinner, reception etc. By having all of the required pictures in a clean checklist form, you can simply hand this sheet to your photographer, (probably in a meeting you will have weeks before your wedding), and you therefore put the onus on your photographer to make sure every picture is taken. Photographers will actually appreciate your organization as they know that once they check off the required pictures you want taken, you should both be satisfied.

Videography – We have a similar spreadsheet for the video portion of your wedding or special event, and the description above applies to this section as well. Remember what we said about asking a relative to do certain aspects for you. If they volunteer, great, if not .....

Music – This spreadsheet follows the format of the ones above. The added benefit is that you are able to add all songs you wish to be played but more importantly those you do not wish to have played during your wedding.

There are also spreadsheets for your florist, caterer and task co-ordinator should you wish to establish these as well.

Event – How do we plan everything we need done?

To control and maintain your Events you will make use of the following *Planning Tools;*

Events and Their Checklists, Calendar, Guests

For any event requiring varying degrees of planning, the Events and Their Checklists tab is the place to start. Simply enter the event you are planning on having with its' associated date and the program will set-up the required planning spreadsheets for you to fill in.

Events Including Wedding & Their Checklists

This is where you add all your wedding related events – **Wedding Ceremony**, **Wedding Reception**, **Engagement Party**, etc......

When you click on the **"Events Including Wedding & Their Checklists"** link you will immediately see your **Wedding Ceremony,** this event is created automatically at sign up. If you have any events that correspond with your wedding ceremony that require a checklist, please click on the **"Event Checklist Link"** next to Wedding Ceremony.

To add another event simply click on the **"Add Event"** Button, notice the field for Event Date and once you have created this event it will automatically show up in your calendar.

The Event Checklist Link – This area has a **Seating Plan, Flowers, Caterer, Videographer, Photographer and Music** checklist in it. Simply click on the link next to any of the categories to add the event checklist to it. This will only work if you have already populated your vendors. Once you have added the checklist and clicked the **Add** button for the event it will automatically show up on the **Event Checklist Page**.

Back to the main Event Checklist Area you will now see a list of your events and links next to your event to **Edit** or **Delete**. There is also a link called **Event Checklist** where you can edit all those things that are on your checklists for that event.

On your program by selecting the "Events and their Checklists" tab you will notice the spreadsheets on the home page of this icon. To manipulate any particular file simply click on the link and that specific file will open. Enter your data where appropriate and you will have created a planning file that can be printed and shared with your suppliers, friends or family.

Using the Karen and Tim's file we can see that two events have been set up. We will use the Wedding Ceremony for the purposes of this example. By selecting the Event Checklists tab, the planning spreadsheets become active.

Select the Event Checklists tab.

Event Checklists Link

Wedding Party or Guest Tasks For Event

In order to work in this section you will have to have filled out your **Vendors.**

You can add tasks that need to be done by either your wedding party or one of your guests. Because there is a date involved with the task it will show up in your "**Calendar**" for easy access and editing.

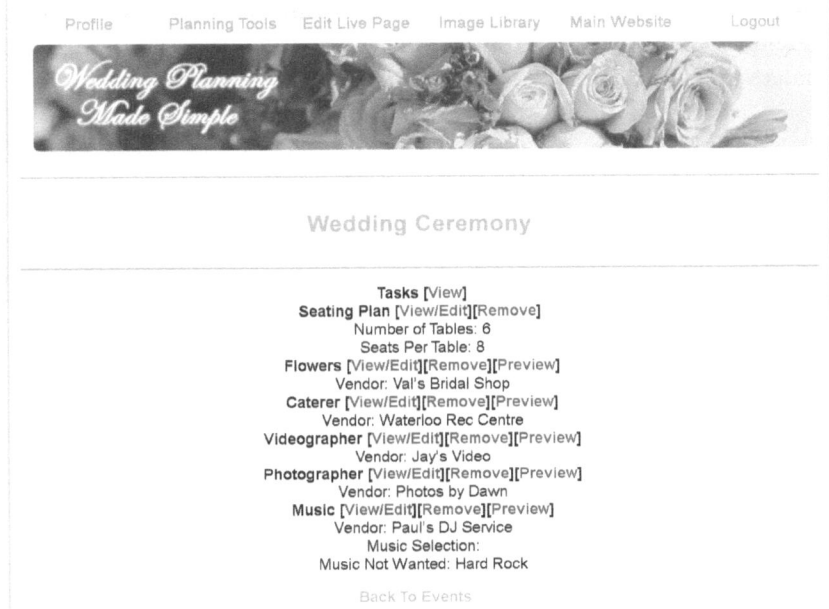

To add a task, simply select the, 'Task [Underline: View]" tab.

As we have mentioned, and the real beauty of using a computer manipulated program, is that by entering a date for a particular task, it automatically populates in your calendar.

Calendar

Anything under your planning tools which has a date will be listed in your personal calendar, you can click on the event or item and edit it directly from your calendar. This is very handy for keeping track of things that need to be completed.

The following charts outline how the rest of the planning tools for this section work.

Flowers

Make sure you have populated your **Vendors** before you work in this area. Click on **Add Flowers**

1. Use your vendor dropdown box to choose your vendor

2. Click the **Add Flower** Button

3. Fill out the **Selection Field,** example **Head Table Centerpiece**

4. Fill out the **Special Request** field if you have one, example **White Roses**

5. Check to make sure your vendor is correct, then click the **Edit Flower** Button

NOTICE – There is an X next to your Flower Fields, this X will delete that section and you can start again.

Now that you have added your floral choices, clicking the **Back to Event** Link will allow you to see your additions on the page. With a new set of menu options, you can click on the **View/Edit** to view or edit your flower choices, use the **Preview** to preview and print your list or you can click on the **Remove** link to totally delete your flower selections and start again.

Caterer

From the Events and Checklists tab, select Caterer (View/Edit), you will be presented with a form
- use the dropdown to find your **Vendor**
- Enter your meal selections
- Enter any comment relating to that selection, (number required, vegetarian etc.)
- Select Update your caterer
- Add another Menu Item

NOTICE – There is an X next to **Menu Item**, this X will delete that section and you can start again.

Now that you have added your caterer choices when you click the **Back to Event** Link, you will see your addition on the page, with a new set of menu options, you can click on the **View/Edit** to view or edit your caterer and food choices, you will see **Preview** where you can preview and print your list or you can click on the **Remove** link to totally delete your caterer and food selections and start again.

Videographer

From the Events and Checklists tab, click the **Add Videographer** link and you are presented with a form, use the dropdown at the top of the page to choose your vendor.

- Fill out the **Video Description** field, example Bride Getting Ready.

- Add another selection by clicking the **Add Video** Button

- Once you have added all your selections, click on the **Edit Video** Button

- You have now saved all your selections and can click on the **Back to Event** link.

- You now have three choices for Videographer, **View/Edit, Remove or Preview**

- You can edit as often as you wish to get your selections perfect.

NOTICE – There is an X next to your Selection, this X will delete that section and you can start again.

Photographer

From the Events and Checklists tab, click on the **Add Photographer** link and you are presented with a form, use the dropdown at the top of the page to choose your vendor.

- Fill out the **Photo Description** field, example Bride Getting Ready.

- Add another selection by clicking the **Add Photo** Button

- Once you have added all your selections, click on the **Edit Photo** Button

- You have now saved all your selections and can click on the **Back to Event** link.

- You now have three choices for Photographer, **View/Edit, Remove or Preview**

- You can edit as often as you wish to get your selections perfect.

NOTICE – There is an X next to your Selection, this X will delete that section and you can add another selection.

Music

Music is a little bit different. For example you can have a quartet for dinner music and a DJ or live band for the reception. You now have the choice to add two or more vendors, after which you can start your lists.

Add Music

When you click on the **Add Music** link you will be presented with a form:

- Use the dropdown next to **Vendor** to choose the vendor
- Fill out **Selection** example **Easy Listening**
- Fill out music not wanted example **Hard Rock or leave blank**
- Click on the **Add Music** Button
- You are now ready to either add another vendor or start adding your music selection.
- To add another Vendor click on the **Add Vendor** Link, another vendor will show up next to your first vendor.
- Follow the instructions above and fill out that new form.
- Then click on the **Add Music** Button

Adding Music Tracks

Once you have saved your **Vendor** by clicking **Add Music** Button (first vendor) or the **Edit Music** Button (second vendor)

- Click the **Add Music Track** Button
- Fill out the Artist
- Fill out the Song, as you know some songs have many artists, make sure you get the right song for your wedding event.
- Fill out the instructions, example First Dance, or Parents Dance etc.
- If you have more than one song, keep adding, but don't forget to click on the **Edit Music** Button to save your selections.

NOTICE – There is an X next to your Selection and your vendor, this X will delete that selection or vendor and you can add another selection.

Seating Plan

This is a handy item which will help you with your wedding guests and head table seating plan.

Click on **Add Seating Plan**

1. Add the number of tables

2. Add seats per table

3. Check either **Assign Guests by Table** or **Assign Guests by Seat** radio button

4. Click on the **Assign Guests** Button

Now you are in the area where you assign your guests to the table or seat.

Adding the Head Table, first things first, you need a Head Table

Click on the **Add Head Table** Link, this will generate a list of people who you have setup as being in your Wedding Party, now you have to put them in your head table.

- Once you have clicked the **Add Head Table Link** notice how it says **Unassigned Guests** above the table

- You now have to assign those guests to either the Bride or the Groom's side

- Example click on one of the names in that table a little box will pop see below

you now have to assign that person to either Bride or Groom by checking the radio button next to the one you choose then just click the **Add Guest** Button

- Depending on what you clicked you will see a table appear that says either **Bride's Side** or **Groom's Side** with that name in it, if you have made a mistake, just click on the **X** next to the person's name and start again.

- Repeat this process until your head table is set up

- You can also add people from your guest list to the head table, click on the **Add Guest to Head Table**, type in Guest Title, example **Flower Girl** then use your dropdown to choose the person from your list, click the **Add Guest** Button and they are now seated at your head table.

Assigning Your Guest by Table or Seat

Once you have finished your head table it is now time to assign the guests a Table or Seat.

- Click on the **Add Guest** Link, the same little box above will pop up except it won't have Guest Title or Bride or Groom side.

- Use the dropdown to choose the guest you want and then click on the **Add Guest** Button, you will now see them added to your table

- Repeat this process until all your guests are seated, if you don't like where you put one of your guests click on the **X** next to their name and remove them.

- You can now add them to their proper table.

- As your guest list starts to fill up, you can rearrange your seating plan until your heart is content.

Now click Generate Seating Plan to Preview and Print your Seating Plan to have a copy handy at all times.

Chapter 5
Stationery

She says...

I knew exactly what I wanted for stationery. I loved the two young kids or 'precious moments' figurines so our wedding theme, including our stationery, was created with that in mind. I was fortunate to have Bryan, being the computer guy that he is, set up the margins and do all the invitations and programs at home. That saved us a significant amount of money. (Albeit he spent a lot of time trying to get the margins to set properly which is probably a big reason for developing this program to give couples a chance to use pre-made templates for their own planning). I had seen friends of mine spend a ton of money on their invitations and be really upset when they found them lying around as garbage on the wedding day once they were no longer required. Remember, as long as the information is correctly stated, few people are going to notice the extra details, money and/or effort you put into your invitations.

He says…

Well I guess it comes as no surprise that when it came to stationery I thought we should do our own. After all, I've heard of some couples spending thousands of dollars on fancy invitations and it just seems as though that money could be better spent elsewhere. While remembering the three questions, in particular, 'What is important to you'?, I know that couples want their invitations to look good, but really what you want is for the information, date of wedding, place, time etc., to be available to all of your guests. When it comes to the question of, 'what is important to your guests', think of where you put invitations for an upcoming wedding when you receive them. Are you the type who puts them, on the fridge, back in the envelope and in the cupboard not opened again until the day of the wedding, or framed and displayed waiting for the big day? What you do is probably what your guests will do, so do you need to spend thousands of dollars on elaborate stationary? If you want to, by all means do so. For those of you wanting to save some money and take pride in doing them yourselves, this chapter is for you. With the quality of computers and printers these days, and the number of wedding specialty stores it is quite possible to create invitations that are not only personalized but hard to distinguish from professional packages. It is also gratifying when you receive compliments on your stationery and you are able to say, 'thank you, we did them ourselves'.

Stationery – What needs to be done?

The purpose of this chapter is not to imply that you need to skimp on your stationery requirements, but to merely present an option to a sometime very expensive portion of your wedding. There are numerous ways to present your invitations to your guests but don't forget what the goal is. Get the information across in a clear and precise manner.

For those who may want some help with the wording we have presented a few samples;

Brides Parents Hosting

Mr. and Mrs. (Bride's Parents Names)
request the honour of your presence
at the marriage of their daughter
First, Middle name (daughter)
To
First, Middle Name (Groom)
Son of
Mr. and Mrs. (Groom's Parents)
Saturday, the 25th of July
Two thousand and Eight at One O'clock
(Location of Ceremony)

Cocktails 5:00 p.m.
Dinner 6:00 p.m.
City Community Centre
Reception to Follow

Both Parents Hosting

Mr. and Mrs. (Bride's Parents Names)
Together with
Mr. and Mrs. (Groom's Parents Names)
request the honour of your presence
at the marriage of their children
First, Middle name (daughter)
and
First, Middle Name (Groom)
Saturday, the 25th of July
Two thousand and Eight at One O'clock
(Location of Ceremony)

Reception to Follow
City Community Centre

(if people are invited to wedding and reception but not dinner)

Couple is Hosting

First, Middle, Last name Bride
and
First, Middle, Last name Groom
request the honour of your presence
at our marriage
Date
at (time)
Location etc.

Combination

First, Middle, Last name Bride
and
First, Middle, Last name Groom
together with
Mr. and Mrs. (Bride's Parents Name)
and
Mr. and Mrs. (Groom's Parents Names)
request the honour of your presence
at their marriage
Date
at (time)
Location etc.

Groom's Parents Hosting

Mr. and Mrs. (Groom's Parents Names)
request the honour of your presence
at the marriage of
First, Middle name (daughter)
to their son
First, Middle Name (Groom)
at (time)
Location etc.

Bride's Mother and Stepfather

Mr. and Mrs. John Smith
request the honour of your presence
at the marriage of Mrs. Smith's daughter

. . .

Bride's Father and Stepmother

Mr. and Mrs. John Smith
request the honour of your presence
at the marriage of Mr. Smith's daughter

. . .

Relative Hosting

Mr. and Mrs. Smith
request the honour of your presence
at the marriage of our granddaughter

. . . .

One Living Parent

Mr. Smith
requests the honour of your presence
at the marriage of his daughter

. . .

or

The honour of your presence is requested
at the marriage of
Julie Smith
daughter of Mr. John Smith and the late Mary Smith

. . . .

Bride's Parents Divorced

Mrs. Jane Smith Johnson
and
Mr. John Johnson
request the honour of your presence
at the marriage of their daughter
Bride's Name

. . . . .

Groom's Parents Divorced

Mr. & Mrs. John Johnson
request the honour of your presence
at the marriage of their daughter
Bride's Name
Groom's Name
son of
Mrs. Jane Smith Campbell
and Mr. John Campbell
……

Stationery – How to get it done?

For those inclined to print or design their own stationery, you will make use of the following *Planning Tools;*

CSV file, Invitations, Guests Lists

We have included samples of invitations that you can use depending on where you buy your stationery. There is a link on your Planning tools to view if your stationery has been uploaded. Finding your template can save you enormous amounts of time with setting printer margins etc. If you want to completely design and print your own, simply follow the instructions below. Also included are instructions of printing your mailing labels.

Wedding Planning Made Simple Create Your Own Invitations & Printing Instructions

---

Printing Invitations With Microsoft™ Word

Making your own event invitations is easy and rewarding, whether you are using special printing software or a regular word processor like Microsoft Word©. Below are seven easy steps to help you print invitations at home on your ink jet or laser printer using Microsoft Word©.

Step One

Measure the width and height of your invitation card. If the invitation folds, measure the open size of the invitation.

Step Two

Open Microsoft Word©. Choose File, then Page Setup. Under the Paper tab, select Custom Size and enter the dimensions of your card.

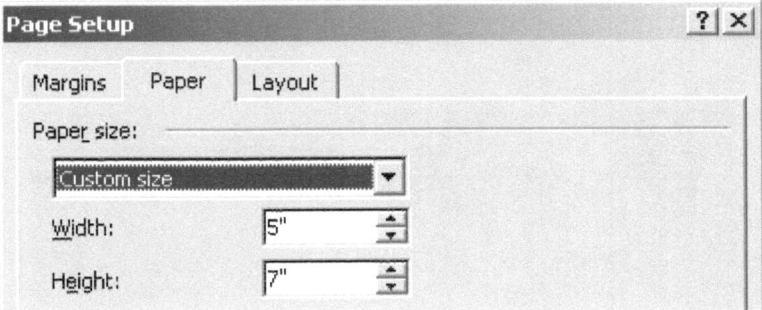

Step Three

Now Select the Margin tab. Here you will select your paper orientation and define the print area. Set your Top, Bottom, Right and Left margins. The margins indicate the distance between the edge of the paper and the type.

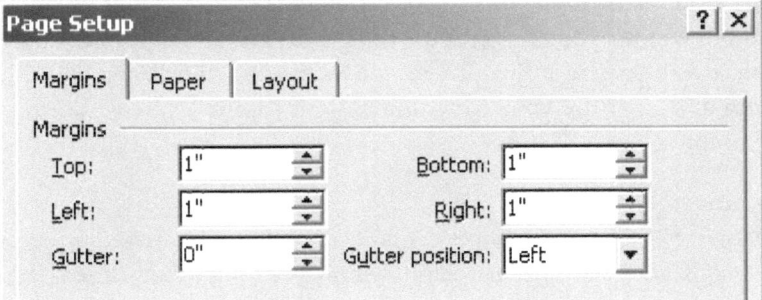

Step Four

On the same tab, select either Portrait (prints the document with the short edge at the top of the page) or Landscape (prints the document with the long edge at the top of the page), from the layout tab.

Step Five

Enter your text. At this point you can choose to insert clipart and/or borders, while making sure that these elements do not interfere with the pre-printed design on the invitation. To insert clipart, choose Insert on the menu, Picture, Clipart..., and browse for a suitable image. To add borders, choose Format, Borders and Shading... and pick a style. Remember to SAVE.

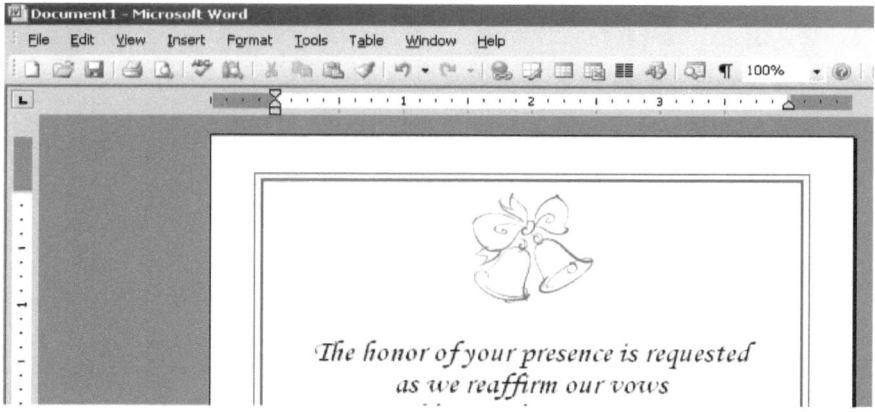

Step Six

From the File menu select Print. If you are using Microsoft Word© 2003, you are ready to continue to Step Seven. If you are using an older version of Microsoft Word©, you must set the printer margins by clicking the Properties button after selecting Print. There you will select the Paper tab. Choose Custom and enter the same paper dimensions that you entered during your page setup.

Step Seven

We suggest first using a test sheet to make certain the text is lined up correctly. Place an "X" on the test sheet before running through the printer. This will help you determine which side faces down. When the text lines up the way you want, you are ready to print your invitations! We suggest printing 10-30 sheets at a time, in order to ensure that the printer does not run out of ink or begin to smudge or crinkle the invitations.

Congratulations, you have now created a professional invitation! Your friends and family will be amazed that you can make your own invitations using your home computer and printer.

You can also go to Avery's Site for free templates, it requires a signup.

By selecting the CSV Icon on your planning tools an Excel© file opens with all of your guests and their contact info. From here you can either send a mass email by selecting, (copy and paste) their email address and sending from your server, or print mailing labels without ever having to re-type their information. You can find instructions on how to print mailing labels on our website.

Chapter 6
Registry & Gifts

She says…

Shopping – who doesn't love shopping? The very thought of registering and planning for all of our requirements as a newly married couple was very exciting. Unfortunately, we were so overwhelmed at the first store that we left without actually completing the registration process. I would recommend going to the store, or stores, first and making a list of the things you want. This way, when you have the, 'gun' in hand, you are ready to select the items you really want.

Also, think about what you really need. We picked out everyday dinnerware as opposed to fine china due to our needs and space constraints. Although my future mother in law thought I would need the china, we selected items that were best for us at the time.

He says...

I like to consider myself to be a very conservative, somewhat bashful individual. I remember feeling guilty even creating a wedding gift list. However, as one family member put it to me,' people will want to buy you something, so you might as well make it easier for them to pick, and better for you to receive if it is something you feel you would like or need for your lives together'.

Now with that said, I wondered how many items I could put on our list from Home Depot or Canadian Tire. It turns out this is probably something that requires some negotiation between you and your future spouse. I am quite certain I have used the hedge trimmer and whipper-snipper, (which I purchased after the wedding), more than those beautiful crystal bowls that I had to build a storage cabinet to hold.

What do you need to be aware of when registering?

When it comes to gifts, think about both giving and receiving. Consider gifts to each other, gifts to the Bridal party and gifts to your parents. As a couple, decide what or who needs to be recognized and when to do this. A rehearsal party is a great time to present gifts, (with the exception of gifts to each other), as it is primarily the people directly involved with your wedding who would attend a function the night before your wedding.

When creating your gift registry, presumably you would use the services of a retail chain which generally have a pretty good system to prepare such a list. Make use of their services and do not be afraid to use multiple stores. You probably already have an idea of what you feel you will require for your new living establishment, and if that requires using the services of many different retailers, so be it.

For heaven's sake, 'don't forget the thank you card'.

How to manage your registry?

To set-up, track and maintain your Registry and Wedding Gifts you will make use of the following *Planning Tools.*

Registry or Wedding Gifts,

We created this section to make it easy for you to track and organize your gifts. Simply enter into a spreadsheet a list of gifts that you would like to receive. Once you receive them, simply check them off, and track which guest or family member purchased it for you. There is also a section where you can highlight if you have sent them a thank you card. Again, 'don't forget the thank you card'.

Registry or Wedding Gifts

In this area, you can list all gifts, whether they are from a Wedding Registry or from your actual Guests. You will be able to track all gifts and also track whether you have sent out a thank you for each gift received.

To add a gift from a Guest

From the "Registry or Wedding Gifts" icon on your planning tools;

- Select the Guests' name
- Gift Description – what the gift is
- Gift From – use the dropdown
- Don't fill out category, that is for Registry Gift
- Store – optional
- Quantity – optional
- Price per item – optional
- Wedding Gift – check this so you know whether it is a wedding gift or registry gift.
- Thank you sent – once you have sent the thank you card, edit this check box

To Add a Registry Gift

- Select the Add/Gift
- Gift Description – what the gift is
- Gift From – use dropdown too choose
- Category – use dropdown, this is your registry categories
- Store – add store
- Quantity – add quantity
- Price per item – add price
- Gift Registry – check this so you know whether it is a wedding gift or registry gift.
- Thank you sent – once you have sent the thank you card, edit this check box

You can edit your gifts at anytime, and filter the list of gifts by **Wedding Gift** or **Registry Gift,** in case your list gets to long.

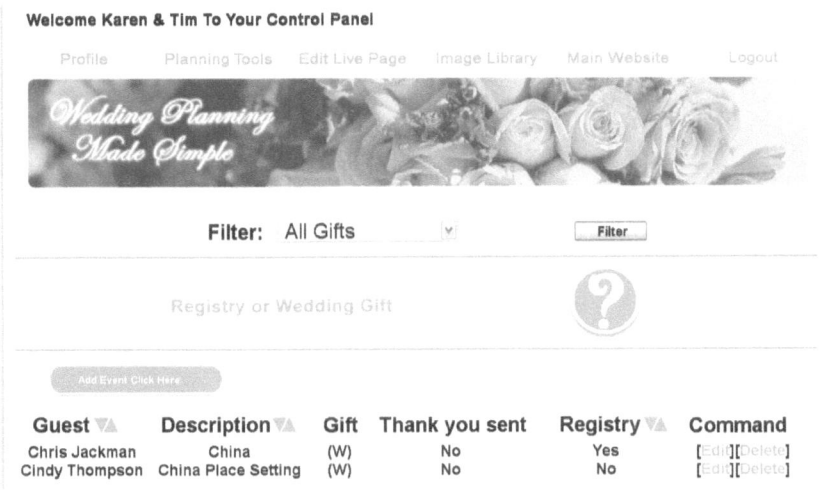

Welcome Karen & Tim To Your Control Panel

Profile   Planning Tools   Edit Live Page   Image Library   Main Website   Logout

Wedding Planning Made Simple

Add/Edit Gift

Gift Description: [   ]

Add Guest
Gift From: [▾]

Add Category
Category: [▾]

Store: [   ]

Quantity: [   ]

Price Per Item: [   ]

Wedding Gift: ☐   Thank You Sent: ☐

Shower Gift: ☐   Thank You Sent: ☐

Gift Registry: ☐

[Update Gift]

Back To Gifts

Chapter 7
Your Personal WebPage

She says…

A wedding website is a great way to share information with friends and family. You can use the website to share your planning as well as share all of your pictures and memories after the wedding. Just be careful to do it safely, making your page private with passwords because you never know who from your past is still looking to see how you are doing.

He says...

When we decided after our wedding that we would pursue the idea of developing a package for other couples taking the plunge, we looked at ways to bring value to our offering. There are numerous planning tools available and we wanted to provide not only the required information but that little extra something that makes people feel they really got their money's worth. With that in mind, we created this Wedding Planner which ties in with our on-line planning program, and topped it off with both a diary and most importantly individual WebPages for every couple. Some of you may use your WebPage as a resource for all of your guests to stay updated, some may use it just to show pictures or special events and some may wish to keep their page private and only available to certain people. The choice is yours, we just wanted to make sure that you had the ability to do what you want with your wedding. Happy planning, relax, have fun and we hope you have the wedding of your dreams.

Your Website – What needs to be done?

The website is pretty straightforward. You are able to add pictures and paragraphs, links and maps or whatever information you want to share with your friends and family. We have provided an option that allows your page to be private. This way, you have to actually contact people and inform them of your site for them to view your page. Alternatively, your page would be viewable by anyone who visited our website. Some couples do not mind, others want the privacy. It is completely up to you.

Building your Wedding Website

To manage your WebPage you will make use of the following *Planning Tools*;

From the top bar of your Control Panel – *Edit Live Page, Image Library*

Use the *Profile* tab if you would like to make your page private. When you select, 'Edit Live Page' you will see the template for your WebPage. On the right hand side there are five tabs.

Add Paragraph – Simply click this tab and you can begin entering your data. You have the ability to alter your text, bold, italic, underscore, change the font family and size, add hyperlinks and change the text colour. Fairly straightforward Word© processing tools.

Save Changes – As its' name suggests, this tab allows you to preserve your work. Don't forget to save any changes you make.

To Control Panel – Should you have to return to the control panel to possibly view some of your other planning programs as you are creating your website this tab allows you to navigate through your program.

Preview – Depressing this tab will allow you to visualize how your webpage will appear to your guests.

Change Template – You have the ability to pick your webpage background. There are five templates you can choose from. Simply pick the style you like and your page will be updated.

Logout – When you are ready to end your session

This is what you will see when you select, 'Edit Live Page' tab.

Adding Pictures

In order to add pictures to your webpage, you will make use of the Image Library tab from the top of your control panel.

Wedding Image Library

- Please note you are allowed to upload 10 images.

- Your image can be a .gif or a .jpg only.

- The maximum allowable size for your image is 500 pixels wide by 500 pixels high or 350 kb (kilobytes).

- This is roughly 5 inches wide.

You will then see an **Upload Image** button. Selecting this will allow you to browse your pictures and chose how your webpage will look.

Diary

For those of you wanting to log your daily or weekly events, the same diary that is presented at the back of this book, is also available on-line.

Diary

Your own personal diary to keep track of all the little extra things that may crop up or simply your feelings on that particular day!

To Use the Diary:

- Use the Calendar to select the date you wish to write about.

- Type in your entry, no need to save, it saves it automatically

- To delete the entry and start again click on the **"Delete Entry"** Link

- To add another entry click on the **"Add Entry"** Button next to the **"View Diary"** Button

- To View your diary click on the **"View Diary"** Button

Our Final Thoughts

We hope that our experiences and this program will alleviate some of the stress that goes along with planning a wedding. Remember, with proper planning you can make your day whatever you want it to be and have lots of fun along the way.

We thought we would take this opportunity to mention a few things we are working on that you may want to use as you go forward with your lives.

If you have any interest in any of the programs listed below, or you have suggestions as we move forward just send an email to info@planingmadesimple. com and we will get you what you need.

What are we working on you ask?

1. We are creating a webpage that you can use after your wedding to share pictures and videos with your friends, (very cheap {probably only $5/ yr} and secure)
2. For about $20 we can create a CD with all of your wedding planning details complete with pictures from your wedding, makes a great keepsake
3. We have access to an inexpensive picture framer. Possible savings of 10-40% off of standard rates
4. We are creating coupon packages that can present hundreds in savings, (coupon package will retail for somewhere between $5-10 with hundreds in savings)
5. While I know it is to early to think about, we are working on a family planning/baby program to help couples

6. We have a financial planning program that is designed to be used in the home to track your personal finances

7. We have options for you to save and even earn commission on any traveling you or your family do, www.jabbs.globaltravel.com is our travel site where you can both save on your travel and earn commissions for any traveling you do.

Plus, we are always adding to our portfolio. Again, if anything above interests you just send us an email (tell us what number(s) interests you,) and we can provide more details.

We, *Bryan and Marian* sincerely thank you for your interest in our product and we wish you all the best with your future endeavors.

Appendix A – 2 year Daily Planner

Here is a little bonus we included with our book. Although we have promoted our on-line wedding planning program there are times when you just need to write things down. That is why we included 24 monthly sheets for you to write down whatever you feel you want to remember or dates that are important to you. Simply write in whatever month you begin to use your diary and simply add the dates as you go along.

Month _____

Monday	Tuesday	Wednesday	Thursday	Friday	Saturday	Sunday

Month _____

Monday	Tuesday	Wednesday	Thursday	Friday	Saturday	Sunday

Month _____

Monday	Tuesday	Wednesday	Thursday	Friday	Saturday	Sunday

Month _____

Monday	Tuesday	Wednesday	Thursday	Friday	Saturday	Sunday

Month _____

Monday	Tuesday	Wednesday	Thursday	Friday	Saturday	Sunday

Month _____

Monday	Tuesday	Wednesday	Thursday	Friday	Saturday	Sunday

Month _____

Monday	Tuesday	Wednesday	Thursday	Friday	Saturday	Sunday

Month _____

Monday	Tuesday	Wednesday	Thursday	Friday	Saturday	Sunday

Month _____

Monday	Tuesday	Wednesday	Thursday	Friday	Saturday	Sunday

Month _____

Monday	Tuesday	Wednesday	Thursday	Friday	Saturday	Sunday

Month _____

Monday	Tuesday	Wednesday	Thursday	Friday	Saturday	Sunday

Month _____

Monday	Tuesday	Wednesday	Thursday	Friday	Saturday	Sunday

Month _____

Monday	Tuesday	Wednesday	Thursday	Friday	Saturday	Sunday

Month _____

Monday	Tuesday	Wednesday	Thursday	Friday	Saturday	Sunday

Month _____

Monday	Tuesday	Wednesday	Thursday	Friday	Saturday	Sunday

Month _____

Monday	Tuesday	Wednesday	Thursday	Friday	Saturday	Sunday

Month _____

Monday	Tuesday	Wednesday	Thursday	Friday	Saturday	Sunday

Month _____

Monday	Tuesday	Wednesday	Thursday	Friday	Saturday	Sunday

Month _____

Monday	Tuesday	Wednesday	Thursday	Friday	Saturday	Sunday

Month _____

Monday	Tuesday	Wednesday	Thursday	Friday	Saturday	Sunday

Month _____

Monday	Tuesday	Wednesday	Thursday	Friday	Saturday	Sunday

Month _____

Monday	Tuesday	Wednesday	Thursday	Friday	Saturday	Sunday

Month _____

Monday	Tuesday	Wednesday	Thursday	Friday	Saturday	Sunday

Month _____

Monday	Tuesday	Wednesday	Thursday	Friday	Saturday	Sunday

Appendix B – Countdown Calendar

Action	Completed
Select Wedding Date	
Determine Particulars (#'s, time etc.)	
Set Budget	
Recordkeeping Method	
Organize Guest List (children?)	
Book Ceremony Site	
Reserve Officiant (pre-marital classes?)	
Book Reception Site	
Select Your Bridal Gown and accessories	
Insert Engagement notice to papers	
Verify or obtain passport etc.	
Select/Book Photographer	

Action	Completed
Select Wedding Party	
Outlines Duties of Wedding Party	
Select Dresses for bridal party	
Book Caterer	
Book Ceremony Musicians	
Book Reception musicians/DJ	
Schedule fittings for dresses	
Book videographer	
Book florist	

4-6 Months Before		*2-4 Months Before*	
Action	**Completed**	**Action**	**Completed**
Wedding Prep Courses (if required)		Select/Order Wedding Cake	
Reserve Rental Items		Order Party favours	
Finalize Guest List		Order decorations	
Select/Order Invitations or Stationery		Select/Book Wedding Transportation	
Reserve Rehearsal particulars		Send Invitations	
Begin Honeymoon arrangements		Purchase Attendant gifts	
Arrange Accommodation for guests		Book hair/make-up appointments	
Register for gifts		Obtain marriage license (check validity,)	
		Design Maps, Directions General info with invitations	
Select/Order wedding rings			
Select Special Readings and Readers		Write wedding vows (if you desire)	
Write Ceremony (if you choose)		Entertainment list for out-of-towners	
		Copies of reading/music to readers	

6-8 Weeks Before		*2-6 Weeks Before*	
Action	**Completed**	**Action**	**Completed**
Record Receipt of gifts/send thank you		Finalize caterer/food and beverages	
Purchase guest book, toasting glasses		Confirm details with officiant	
Reserve Attire for Groomsmen		Arrange final fittings	
Set rehearsal time and date		Finalize floral arrangements	

Buy attendant's gifts

Prepare schedule/agenda for reception

Buy bride and groom presents (if you choose)

Discuss Photography wishes

Videography Wishes

Determine Reception seating plan

Ensure honeymoon details

Dinner seating arrangements (if you desire)

1 Week Before

Action	Completed
Verify numbers with reception/caterer	
Verify transportation	
Contact all vendors (just to check)	

Rehearsal Day

Action	Completed
Drop off decorations at reception site	
Make sure you have all gifts	
Payments for all parties are taken care of	
Pack for wedding night/ honeymoon	
Rehearsal	
Review Ceremony	

Wedding Day

Action	Completed
Ensure all items are where they need to be	
Rings to best man or maid of honour	
Enjoy Your day	

Appendix C – Quick Start Guide and Easy Help File References

Quick Start

This will briefly explain the steps you should take to start using your planning tools:

1. Make Sure Your **Profile** is filled out with the correct **Budget Amount**

2. Make sure you have filled out your Expense Categories & Percent of Budget - this area is the list of Expense Categories you will have for anything relating to your wedding example Caterers, Florist, Limousine, Bakery, Music, Photographer, Videographer etc..... Don't forget to add what percent of the budget you have allocated for the **Category** when you fill this out also please make sure your budget adds up to 100 percent, you can always go in and edit the percent of budget you wish to allocate for each category as time goes on.

3. Make sure you have filled out your Vendors list, your vendor list is the list of companies performing a service at any of your wedding related functions, example: 123 Florist Ltd., My Music Inc., 123 Video Productions

4. Next you should fill out your **Guest List**, which includes your wedding party, we have put this in one area for your convenience.

IMPORTANT Your **Expense Category** and your **Vendors List** are two separate things, one is a **Category** example: Music, Video, Photography, Caterer, the other is the actual **Company Performing the Service** example: 123 Florist Ltd., My Music Inc., 123 Video Productions, etc etc....

Anything that you fill out that has a dollar amount in the form field will show up in your **Budget

Anything you fill out that has a date field will show up in your **Calendar

** There are individual help files for each section look for the
question mark and click on it for help relating to that screen.

Help Files For Wedding Planning Made Simple

NOTE: When your account was created, we automatically created an event called

Wedding Ceremony which can be accessed in "Events Including Wedding & Their Checklists"

NOTE: We have added your **Wedding Ceremony**, you will still have to add your **Wedding Reception** as a separate event in order to add seating plans, flowers, music, photography etc...

Profile

This is where you:

- Edit your profile

- Add or edit your budget amount

- Update or change your wedding date

- Change your password.

Planning Tools

This section is where you do all your wedding planning. Below is a detailed explanation of how to use all the tools available in this area.

Guest List

This is where you can add your guest list and the people in your wedding party.

By clicking on the "**Add Guest**" Button you simply fill out the form, check if they are in the wedding party or not, if they are, type in their title, for example **Bridesmaid** or **Flower Girl,** and the program takes care of the rest. For guests simply type in their particulars.

Come back to this area when your guest has sent you their R.S.V.P., click on the "**Edit**" link next to the guest name and check the R.S.V.P. box "**Yes**", and then click the "**Edit Guest**" Button to update your guest.

You can also delete a guest from the list by clicking on the **Delete** link under the heading Command

Once you have added a guest, go back to the main guest page and you can edit or delete your guest, you can also change them from a **Guest** to **Wedding Party** member or visa-versa.

Budget

Now that you have set your budget amount in your **Profile** area, you can click on **Budget or the Budget Icon** and look for the link that says **"Change Budget Amount"** should you wish edit or change your budget amount. The "**Individual Expense Category**" on your planning tools page populates all your budget information.

NOTE - Make sure you have filled out all your **Vendors** and your **Expense Categories** before you attempt to do your Individual Expenses. **And also make sure your categories add up to 100% together for an accurate forecast.**

Vendors

Vendors are all the suppliers that will be providing you with items for your events, like your **Wedding Reception**, your **Wedding Ceremony**, your **Buck & Doe** etc....

In this area you add a vendor, which then populates the main vendor page. Once you see it on the main vendor page you can edit or delete this vendor. You can also add any notes you need to keep track of about this vendor.

Expense Category & Percent of Budget - Plus Registry Categories

This is broken into two areas.

- **Expense Categories**

- **Registry Categories**

Expense Categories

In this area you add all your different **Expense Categories** and what percent of the budget they will take up, example **Limousine Service** or **Videographer** or **Photographer** and what percent of the budget you would like to allow for these categories**.**

How to add an Budget Expense Category - click on the **Add Budget Category** Button, a little box will pop up asking you for a **Category Name** and **Percent of Budget**, if you aren't sure just fill out the Category Name, you can always come back and add the percent of budget later, click on the

Add Category Name Button, now you will see your new category under the **Budget Categories** heading. You can edit or delete these at any time.

Please make sure your categories add up to 100% together for an accurate forecast.

Individual Expenses

NOTE - Make sure you have filled out all your **Vendors** and your **Expense Categories** before you attempt to do your Expenses.

Adding an individual Expense :

- description
- vendor
- category
- total amount - (shows up under budget)
- amount paid so far - (shows up under budget)
- deposit
- delivery date - (shows up in your calendar, anything with a date will show up in your calendar)

Don't forget to update your payments made on your expenses, under the **Edit** link

Accounts Payable

This area shows you all your expenses that you have entered, with your;

- Vendor
- Cost
- Deposit
- Amount Paid
- Amount left
- Whether it is completed or not

You can also filter the results you view on this page by category or vendor and by expense fully paid or to be paid. Additionally you can click on the **pink expense title** to edit the expense directly from this page.

Contacts

This area lists all your contacts including your **Vendors, Wedding Guests** and **Wedding Party.**

You can display all your contacts at once or display them by **Vendor, Wedding Guest** or **Wedding Party** in-case your lists get to long. You can also click on a contact and directly update them from this area. This area is all your contacts at a glance.

Events Including Wedding & Their Checklists

This is where you add all your wedding related events - **Wedding Ceremony**, **Wedding Reception**, **Buck & Doe**, etc......

When you click on the **"Events Including Wedding & Their Checklists"** link you will immediately see your **Wedding Ceremony,** this event is created automatically at sign up. If you have any events that correspond with your wedding ceremony that require a checklist, please click on the **"Event Checklist Link"** next to Wedding Ceremony.

To add another event simply click on the "**Add Event**" Button, notice the field for Event Date and once you have created this event it will automatically show up in your calendar.

The Event Checklist Link - This area has a **Seating Plan, Flowers, Food, Videographer, Photographer and Music** checklist in it. Simply click on the link next to any of the categories to add the event checklist to it. This will only work if you have already populated your vendors. Once you have added the checklist and clicked the **Add** button for the event it will automatically show up on the **Event Checklist Page**.

Back to the main Event Checklist Area you will now see a list of your events and links next to your event to **Edit** or **Delete.** There is also a link called **Event Checklist** where you can edit all those things that are on your checklists for that event.

Event Checklists Link

Wedding Party or Guest Tasks For Event

In order to work in this section you will have to have filled out your **Vendors.**

You can add tasks that need to be done by either your wedding party or one of your guests. Because there is a date involved with the task it will show up in your "**Calendar**" for easy access and editing.

Seating Plan

This is a handy item which will help you with your wedding guests and head table seating plan.

Click on **Add Seating Plan**

1. Add the number of tables

2. Add seats per table

3. Check either **Assign Guests by Table** or **Assign Guests by Seat** radio button

4. Click on the **Assign Guests** Button

Now you are in the area where you assign your guests to the table or seat.

Adding the Head Table, first things first, you need a Head Table

Click on the **Add Head Table** link, this will generate a list of people who you have set up as being in your Wedding Party. Now you have to put them in your head table.

*   Once you have clicked the **Add Head Table Link** notice how it says **Unassigned Guests** above the table

*   You now have to assign those guests to whatever side you like, the Bride or the Groom

*   Example: click on one of the names in that table and a little box will pop see below

- you now have to assign that person to either Bride or Groom by checking the radio button next to the one you choose

- then just click the **Add Guest** Button

- Depending on what you clicked you will see a table appear that says either **Bride's Side** or **Groom's Side** with that name in it, if you have made a mistake, just click on the **X** next to the person's name and start again.

- Repeat this process until your head table is set up

- You can also add people from your guest list to the head table, click on the **Add Guest to Head Table**, type in Guest Title, example **Flower Girl** then use your dropdown to choose the person from your list, click the **Add Guest** Button and they are now seated at your head table.

Assigning Your Guest by Table or Seat

Once you have finished your head table it is now time to assign the guests a Table or Seat.

- Click on the **Add Guest** Link, the same little box above will popup except it won't have Guest Title or Bride or Groom side.

- Use the dropdown to choose the guest you want then click on the **Add Guest** Button you will now see them added to your table

- Repeat this process until all your guests are seated, if you don't like where you put one of your guests click on the **X** next to their name and remove them.

- You can now add them to the proper table.

- As your guest list starts to fill up, you can rearrange your seating plan until your heart is content.

Now click Generate Seating Plan to Preview and Print your Seating Plan to have a copy handy at all times.

Notice the **X** next to each Person at the head table except the Bride and Groom, you can delete any member of the wedding party, you can also add additional people to the head table for instance a **Flower Girl** or **Ring Bearer**, just make sure you have added them in your **Guest List** Area then when you click the **Add Guest To Head Table** Link a box appears fill it out choose your guest and click the **Add Guest** Button, voila, they are added.

Flowers

Make sure you have populated your **Vendors** before you work in this area. Click on **Add Flowers**

1. Use your vendor dropdown box to choose your vendor

2. Click the **Add Flower** Button

3. Fill out the **Selection Field,** example **Head Table Centerpiece**

4. Fill out the **Special Request** field if you have one, example: **White Roses**

5. Check to make sure your vendor is correct, then click the **Edit Flower** Button

NOTICE - There is an X next to your Flower Fields, this X will delete that section and you can start again.

Now that you have added your floral choices when you click the **Back to Event** Link, you will see your addition on the page, with a new set of menu options, you can click on the **View/Edit** to view or edit your flower choices, you will see **Preview** where you can preview and print your list or you can click on the **Remove** link to totally delete your flower selections and start again.

Caterer

When you click on **Add Caterer** you will be presented with a form, use the dropdown to find your **Vendor** then for selections you add the type of meals that you plan on having at your function, for instance, you can add vegetarian meals and in the comments area you can add 30 needed, or you can add chicken with vegetables and potatoes the comment can be, gravy included.

NOTICE - There is an X next to **Menu Item**, this X will delete that section and you can start again.

Now that you have added your caterer choices when you click the **Back to Event** Link, you will see your addition on the page, with a new set of menu options, you can click on the **View/Edit** to view or edit your caterer and food choices, you will see **Preview** where you can preview and print your list or you can click on the **Remove** link to totally delete your caterer and food selections and start again.

Videographer

When you click on the **Add Videographer** link you will be presented with a form, use the dropdown at the top of the page to choose your vendor.

- Fill out the **Video Description** field, example Bride Getting Ready.

- Add another selection by clicking the **Add Video** Button

- Once you have added all your selections and you are happy, click on the **Edit Video** Button

- You have now saved all your selections and can click on the **Back to Event** link.

- You now have three choices for Videographer, **View/Edit, Remove or Preview**

- You can edit as often as you wish to get your selections perfect.

NOTICE - There is an X next to your Selection, this X will delete that section and you can start again.

Now that you have added your video choices when you click the **Back to Event** Link, you will see your addition on the page, with a new set of menu options, you can click on the **View/Edit** to view or edit your video, you will see **Preview** where you can preview and print your list or you can click on the **Remove** link to totally delete your video selections and start again.

Photographer

When you click on the **Add Photographer** link you will be presented with a form, use the dropdown at the top of the page to choose your vendor.

- Fill out the **Photo Description** field, example Bride Getting Ready.

- Add another selection by clicking the **Add Photo** Button

- Once you have added all your selections and you are happy, click on the **Edit Photo** Button

- You have now saved all your selections and can click on the **Back to Event** link.

- You now have three choices for Photographer, **View/Edit, Remove or Preview**

- You can edit as often as you wish to get your selections perfect.

NOTICE - There is an X next to your Selection, this X will delete that section and you can add another selection.

Now that you have added your video choices when you click the **Back to Event** Link, you will see your addition on the page, with a new set of menu options, you can click on the **View/Edit** to view or edit your video, you will see **Preview** where you can preview and print your list or you can click on the **Remove** link to totally delete your video selections and start again.

Music

Music is a little bit different say for example you have a quartet for dinner music and a DJ or live band for the reception. You now have the choice to add two or more vendors, then you can start your lists from there.

Add Music

When you click on the **Add Music** link you will be presented with a form:

- Use the dropdown next to **Vendor** to choose the vendor

- Fill out **Selection** example: **Easy Listening**

- Fill out music not wanted example: **Hard Rock or leave blank**

- Click on the **Add Music** Button

- You are now ready to either add another vendor or start adding your music selection.

- To add another Vendor click on the **Add Vendor** Link another vendor will show up next to your first vendor.

- Follow the instructions above and fill out that new form.

- Then click on the **Add Music** Button

Adding Music Tracks

- Once you have saved your **Vendor** by clicking **Add Music** Button, (first vendor), or the **Edit Music** Button, (second vendor)

- Click the **Add Music Track** Button

- Fill out the Artist

- Fill out the Song, as you know some songs have many artists, make sure you get the right song for your wedding event.

- Fill out the instructions, example: First Dance, or Parents Dance etc.

- If you have more than one song, keep adding, but don't forget to click on the **Edit Music** Button to save your selections.

NOTICE - There is an X next to your Selection and your vendor, this X will delete that selection or vendor and you can add another selection.

Now that you have added your vendors and music choices when you click the **Back to Event** Link, you will see your addition on the page, with a new set of menu options, you can click on the **View/Edit** to view or edit your music, you will see **Preview** where you can preview and print your list or you can click on the **Remove** link to totally delete your music selections and start again.

Calendar

Anything under your planning tools which has a date will be listed in your personal calendar. You can click on the event or item and edit it directly from your calendar. This is very handy for keeping track of things that need to be completed.

Registry or Wedding Gifts

In this area you can list all gifts, whether they are from a Wedding Registry or from your actual Guest. You will be able to track all gifts and also track whether you have sent out a thank you for each gift received.

To add a gift from a Guest

- Gift Description - what the gift is
- Gift From - use the dropdown
- Don't fill out category, that is for Registry Gift
- Store - optional
- Quantity - optional
- Price per item - optional
- Wedding Gift - check this so you know whether it is a wedding gift or registry gift.
- Thank you sent - once you have sent the thank you card, edit this check box

To Add a Registry Gift

- Gift Description - what the gift is
- Gift From - use dropdown to choose

- Category - use dropdown, this is your registry categories
- Store - add store
- Quantity - add quantity
- Price per item - add price
- Gift Registry - check this so you know whether it is a wedding gift or registry gift.
- Thank you sent - once you have sent the thank you card, edit this check box

You can edit your gifts at anytime, and filter the list of gifts by **Wedding Gift** or **Registry Gift,** in-case your list gets too long.

Diary

Your own personal diary to keep track of all the little extra things that may crop up or simply your feelings on that particular day!

To Use the Diary:

- Use the Calendar to select the date you wish to write about.
- Type in your entry, no need to save, it saves it automatically
- To delete the entry and start again click on the **"Delete Entry"** Link
- To add another entry click on the **"Add Entry"** Button next to the **"View Diary"** Button
- To View your diary click on the **"View Diary"** Button

Appendix D – Setting Up Your On-Line Program

Thank you once again for your interest in our program and we truly wish you all the best with your upcoming nuptials and lives together.

Just a quick start guide to accessing your program;

To begin using your on-line program, including your webpage simply do the following;

Email us at **weddingbook@planningmadesimple.com** and provide us with your name, wedding date and proof of purchase. You will receive a return email with instructions and link to set up your account. You will also receive an access code that you use to verify authenticity.

Please include in the email the store you purchased this book at and the UPC label code from the cover of the book, or receipt number from your vendor. Once we verify your information we will set up your account. Please allow 24 hours for the activation to take place.

If you have any questions please contact us at info@planningmadesimple.com

Regards,

PlanningMadeSimple

Notes:

Notes:

Contacts:

www.ingramcontent.com/pod-product-compliance
Lightning Source LLC
Chambersburg PA
CBHW020253290526
45784CB00003B/1230